A Cafecito Story

A Cafecito Story

JULIA ALVAREZ

Afterword by BILL EICHNER

Woodcuts by BELKIS RAMÍREZ

CHELSEA GREEN PUBLISHING COMPANY
White River Junction, Vermont

Designed by Ann Aspell.

Printed in China.
First printing, September 2001

04 03 02 01   1 2 3 4 5

Library of Congress Cataloging-in-Publication Data

Alvarez, Julia.
  A cafecito story / Julia Alvarez ; afterword by Bill Eichner.
    p. cm.
  ISBN 1-931498-00-8 (alk. paper)
    1. Americans—Dominican Republic—Fiction. 2. Agriculture,
Cooperative—Fiction. 3. Dominican Republic—Fiction. 4. Organic
Farming—Fiction. 5. Coffee growers—Fiction. I. Title.
PS3551.L845 C3 2001
813'.54—dc21   2001047092

Chelsea Green Publishing Company
Post Office Box 428
White River Junction, VT 05001
(800) 639-4099
www.chelseagreen.com

John Gilbert Eichner
1919–2001

Ruth Marie Eichner
1918–2001

who taught us to love the land
deeper our love
now that you are a part of it

A

J OE grew up on a farm in Nebraska dreaming of following in his father's footsteps and becoming a farmer. It was a hard life with sweet moments, many of the sweetest in the company of birds.

Early spring, Joe would plant corn, trying to keep his rows as straight as his father's. White gulls swirled around his tractor, occasionally swooping down to pick grubs from the tilled soil. Sea gulls, everyone called them.

Every time they did so, they distracted the young Joe. His dad used to say that he could read the heartbeat of his son's attention from the zigzags in his row. But Joe couldn't stop wondering where those gulls had come from. Nebraska is a long ways from the sea.

With the heat of summer came the long, back-breaking days of haying. Joe would stack the ninety-pound bales in the loft of the barn. The only company in that hot spot under the roof were barn swallows and sparrows sailing through the door to their nests and pigeons sitting on the rafters cooing to each other while they watched him sweat.

But the small farms started to go under. By the time Joe was a young man, his dad had to sell off most of his land to pay the bills. Farming became a business run by people in offices who had never put their hands in the soil. Joe decided this was not for him.

The school counselor suggested teaching instead. After all, Joe loved to read and talk about what he had read.

So, Joe ended up in the classroom. Putting books in his students' hands was not all that different from sowing seeds in a field. Still, something seemed to be missing from his life.

Early mornings, in his rented apartment, he would sit at his desk, reading a book, sipping a strong cup of coffee. Sometimes, he'd look out over the fields that his father had once owned and farmed. Computerized projections now determined the size of the harvest before the seeds were in the ground. The rows were all uniform. The gulls, gone.

4

Years went by. The fields outside Joe's windows became parking lots and housing developments, small malls with big chain stores. The coffee he drank got fancier. Beans from all over the world. The rents higher. The loneliness deeper.

Joe married a city girl and moved to Omaha. But the marriage didn't take. For years, Joe kept to himself, following his routines, but still feeling adrift, a little lost. Finally, one Christmas, he decided to take off. A vacation might help him get out of the rut he was in.

It being winter, it being Nebraska, he thought of the tropics. Searching the Web, he discovered all kinds of resort packages, photos showing barely clad beauties tossing beach balls with waves sounding in the background.

That's just what he needed. Some time to figure out where he was going, maybe mend a broken heart with a new romance—and get a suntan in the bargain.

Joe browsed for hours, sipping his cup of coffee.

He found a great deal: *Dominican Republic: the land Columbus loved the best* . . . Joe clicked and typed and pressed, and in a few minutes, he was confirmed on a package vacation to the lap of happiness.

B

J OE packs a suitcase full of more books than he can possibly read in two weeks, including his old Spanish textbook and dictionary. He means to brush up on his high-school Spanish.

Me llamo Joe. Soy maestro. Mi papá era agricultor.

Pretty good, he thinks, for a gringo going on forty.

On the plane, Joe pictures himself wandering down a sandy beach, a book in hand. Just ahead, a barely clad beauty tosses a beach ball in the air. . . .

He has been spending too much time in cyberspace.

Joe turns on his reading light and opens his Spanish book to the chapter on irregular verbs. *Saber, soñar, surgir.* To know, to dream, to rise.

Closing his eyes, Joe hears the drone of the engines and a faint whistling as if birdsong were being piped through the air vents.

The beach resort is surrounded by a high wall, guards at the entrances, checking ID cards. No natives are allowed on the grounds except the service people who wear Aunt Jemima kerchiefs and faux-Caribbean costumes and perpetual, desperate smiles of welcome.

The barely clad beauties come with men already attached to their arms.

Joe gets through two novels in as many days.

By the third morning, Joe has had enough. He wanders out of the compound to a roadside barra where the locals stop for coffee on their way to work. No long menu of options to choose from. Coffee comes in one denomination: a dollhouse-sized cup filled with a delicious, dark brew that leaves stains on the cup. Joe closes his eyes and concentrates on the rich taste of the beans. He hears the same faint whistle he heard on the plane, getting closer.

When he is done, the barra owner's wife asks him if he wants his future told. Joe nods and holds out his hand.

No, the woman explains. Turn your cup over, and let it drain.

Joe does so, and the woman studies the stains, her eyes narrowed.

I see mountains, she says, pointing. I see a new life. I see many, many birds.

Do you see another cup of coffee? Joe asks, smiling. Fill her up.

From the owner of the barra, Joe finds out that there are coffee farms in the mountains of the interior. In fact, the barra owner has a cousin, Miguel, who grows coffee in his small parcela up near Manabao close to Pico Duarte. Joe has read about Pico Duarte: *The tallest peak east of the Mississippi on the northern half of the hemisphere.*

Why not go there for the weekend?

I told you I saw mountains, the barra owner's wife reminds him.

The resort offers an inland package—a flight by helicopter, a circling of the peak, a champagne picnic at the base camp, then back in time for the evening happy hour. Would he like to sign up?

No gracias. Instead, Joe takes a public guagua, a pickup truck filled with campesinos and their chickens and hogs and goats. He pays 10 pesos, about 50 cents, for the ride to the mountains. At a roadside comedor, he eats a lunch called the Dominican flag: rice and beans and a little piece of beef on the side, for 35 pesos.

He gets to practice his high-school Spanish for free.

As the truck heads up the narrow, curving road, Joe notices the brown mountainsides, ravaged and deforested, riddled with gullies. The road is made even more narrow by huge boulders. They must roll down during rainstorms. No trees to hold back the eroding soil.

Suddenly, the hillsides turn a crisp, metallic green. A new variety of coffee grown under full sun, the old man beside him explains. A young man with a kerchief over his mouth is spraying the leaves.

¿Qué es? Joe asks the old man.

Veneno, he answers, clutching his throat. A word Joe doesn't have to look up in his dictionary. Poison.

Joe finds Miguel's farm. You can't miss it. In the midst of the green desert, Miguel's land is filled with trees. Tall ones tower over a spreading canopy of smaller ones. Everywhere there are bromeliads and birdsong. A soft light falls on the thriving coffee plants.

Perched on a branch, a small thrush says its name over and over again, chinchilín-chinchilín. A flock of wild parrots wheel in the sky as if they are flying in formation, greeting him.

Miguel's house is made of pinewood, the roof is zinc, the door is opened. There are no electric wires, no telephone poles. Miguel smiles in welcome, half a dozen kids around him. Carmen, his wife, is out back, boiling rábanos for their supper.

A buen tiempo, Miguel says. You have come at a good time.

Supper is a bowl of víveres, the boiled roots that the family is accustomed to eating in the evenings. Afterwards, Joe

learns about Miguel's farm, planted with coffee the old way, under shade trees that offer natural protection to the plants, filtering the sun and the rain, feeding the soil and preventing erosion. Not to mention attracting birds that come to sing over the cherries.

That makes for a better coffee, Miguel explains. When a bird sings to the cherries as they are ripening, it is like a mother singing to her child in the womb. The baby is born with a happy soul.

The shaded coffee will put that song inside you, Miguel continues. The sprayed coffee tastes just as good if you are tasting only with your mouth. But it fills you with the poison swimming around in that dark cup of disappointment.

So why doesn't everyone farm coffee in the old way? Joe asks.

The new way you can plant more coffee, you don't have to wait for trees, you can have quicker results, you can have more money in your pocket.

Miguel keeps pointing at Joe when he says "you."

The next morning, Miguel shows Joe the line on the mountain where the shaded coffee ends and the green desert begins. He and his small farmer neighbors are about to cave in and rent their plots and grow coffee for the company using the new techniques.

15

La compañía has the mercado, Miguel explains. If we work for them we will get 80 pesos a day, 150 if we are willing to spray the poison. I get 35 pesos for a caja of beans, Carmen can pick two cajas a day. It takes three years for me to get a coffee harvest. On the plantation, with their sprays, they have coffee in a year.

Sipping his coffee, Joe becomes aware of how much labor has gone into this feast of flavors, how little trickles down to the small farmer. But an idea is percolating in his head. What Miguel needs to do is write his story down, spread the word, so coffee drinkers everywhere will learn of his plight.

I cannot do that, Miguel says quietly. I do not know my letters.

Later that morning, Joe tests Miguel's kids. Standing in the vivero where the new plants are growing, he asks them to scratch their names in the soil with a stick. They shake their heads shyly. The little one, Miguelina, takes the stick and draws a circle on the ground, then looks up smiling, as if her name is zero.

By evening, Joe has decided to spend his whole vacation up in the mountains.

All day, he works alongside Miguel and his children. At night, as he reads, he looks up and sees the family watching him.

What is it the paper says? Miguel wants to know.

Stories, Joe explains. Stories that help me understand what it is to be alive on this earth.

Miguel looks down at the book in Joe's hands with new respect and affection. Joe has noticed this same look on Miguel's face as he inspects the little coffee plants in his vivero.

Every day as they work together, Miguel tells Joe the story of coffee.

How before the coffee can be planted, the land must be prepared in terraces with trees of differing heights to create layers of shade: first, cedros; then, guamas and banana trees.

Meanwhile, Miguel starts the coffee seeds in a germination bed. It takes about fifty days for the shoots to come up.

From the germination bed, the little transplants go into a vivero for eight months. Finally, when they are bold and strong, Miguel plants them on the terraces.

Then comes the weeding and the feeding of the plants with abonos made from whatever there is around. We say orgánico, Miguel explains, because we use only what nature provides for free.

After three years, si Dios quiere, we have a first harvest. We pick four times during the season which goes from December to March. Only the red cherries, of course.

Then the rush is on: we must depulp the cherry that same night or early the next morning. The pulp goes to our worm bed where we are producing our natural fertilizers.

The wet granos, we take to the river for washing. They must be bathed with running water for eight or so hours— a watchful process, as we have to get the bean to just that moment when the grains are washed but no fermentation has begun. It is not unlike that moment with a woman— Miguel smiles, looking off toward the mountains—when love sets in.

And then, the long drying process in the sun. Some of us, who cannot afford a concrete patio, use the paved road. The grains have to be turned every four hours. At night, we pile them up and bring them under cover. Woe to us if there is rain and we do not get our granos covered quickly enough! Wet coffee molds and ends up in the abono pile.

After about two weeks, if the weather is good, we bag the coffee—

Joe sighs with relief. I didn't realize so much work went into one cup! he confesses.

I am not finished, Miguel continues, holding up a hand. Once the coffee is bagged, we let it rest. A few days, a few weeks. We have only taken off the pulp but the bean is still inside the pergamino. So, after the rest, we haul the bags down to the beneficio to have this pergamino removed. Then we sort the beans very carefully by hand, since one sour bean in a bag can spoil the taste for the buyer. The seconds we keep for ourselves.

You mean to tell me that great coffee I've been drinking is seconds? Joe asks, shaking his head.

Miguel nods. The export grade is, of course, for export.

But your coffee is so much better than anything I've tasted in fancy coffee shops in Omaha, Joe notes.

That is because—as you told me yourself—you are a farmer's son, Miguel explains. You taste with your whole body and soul.

Until this moment of Miguel saying so, Joe did not know this was true. He remembers his father planting corn in rows so straight, God Himself might have drawn the lines with a

ruler. While he worked, Joe's father would whistle a little tune as if he were in conversation with a flock of invisible birds.

Sometimes, as Joe works alongside Miguel, he finds himself whistling that same tune.

You can't sell your land! Joe tells Miguel that evening. You need to keep planting coffee your old way. You need to save this bit of the earth for your children and for all of us. You've got to convince your neighbors before it is too late.

Easy enough for you to say, Miguel says. You don't have to live this struggle.

That night, Joe decides.

The next morning, he rides the truck down with farmers and chickens and goats and hogs. In town, he enters the Codetel trailer and dials the place he used to call home.

Joe buys a parcela next to Miguel's. They make a pact. They will not rent their plots to the compañía and cut down their trees. They will keep to the old ways. They will provide a better coffee.

And, Joe adds, you will learn your letters. I myself will teach you.

Every day, under Miguel's gentle direction, Joe learns how to grow coffee. They make terraces and plant trees.

Every night, under the light of an oil lamp, Miguel and his family learn their ABCs. They write letters and read words.

By the time Miguel and Carmen and their children have learned to write their names, the little seeds have sprouted. When the trees are a foot high, the family has struggled through a sentence. All of them can read a page by the time

the trees reach up to Miguel's knees. When the coffee is as tall as little Miguelina, they have progressed to chapters. In three years, by the time of the first coffee harvest from trees Joe has planted, Miguel and Carmen and their children can read a whole book.

It is amazing how much better coffee grows when sung to by birds or when through an opened window comes the sound of a human voice reading words on paper that still holds the memory of the tree it used to be.

Miguel and Joe's idea spreads. Many of the small farmers join them, banding together into a cooperativo and building their own beneficio for processing the beans rather than having to pay high fees to use the compañía facilities. They can now read the contracts the buyers bring and argue for better terms. Joe buys books in the ciudad where he goes periodically to ship the cooperativo coffee to the United States. Carmen cooks for the workers and adds eggs from her hens or cheese from her goats to the bowl of víveres she serves her family at night. More hens and more goats mean more abono for the coffee plants. Miguelina no longer makes a zero when she is asked to write her name.

The years go by. The hillsides are full of songbirds, the cedros are tall and elegant, the guama trees full, the cherries bright red, and the hair on Joe's head is turning white, which is natural when you are fifty-five.

For his fifty-fifth Christmas, Joe decides to visit Nebraska. Over the years, his brothers and sisters and their children have visited the farm-cooperativo, but Joe has never gone back.

Superintendent would boil me alive in a vat of coffee, he jokes when his sister suggests a visit. Remember, I left that teaching job mid-year.

Don't worry, his sister tells him. When you called mid-year, saying you wouldn't be back, the super was only too glad to get rid of a young radical.

I was a young radical? Joe asks.

In Nebraska you were. After all, you liked reading more than football. Oh, please come, Joey, his sister adds. I hate the thought of you all alone at Christmas without your family.

I have a family, Joe explains. Although he has never married, he has become a husband to the land. He is surrounded by his large campesino familia, all of whom he has taught to read and write.

But still, a man needs to go back to where he started from and take a look around.

C

J OE barely recognizes his hometown in Nebraska. There are a lot more houses, a new mall, a truck stop, a strip of fast-food chains. Beside the Dunkin' Donuts is a holdout, an old, frame house with its name—*Early Bird Cafe*—written in curlicue script on the glass. Joe stops there his first morning for a cup of coffee.

As he steps inside, a little bell tinkles. A woman at the counter looks up from the book she's reading. She is in her early forties, Joe guesses, with dark hair and eyes the color of coffee beans.

Howdy, he says. Can I bother you for a cafecito?

The woman puts her book away reluctantly. Say what? she asks him.

Joe smiles. That's Spanish for a cup of coffee.

The woman serves him a cup that Joe can barely get down.

Where'd you get this coffee? Joe asks.

Supplier, the woman replies. Is there something wrong with it?

Joe nods. Remember that book you were reading when I walked in the door? Held your imagination. A cup of coffee has to do the same thing. So, to answer your question, this cup of coffee is like a book you end up using as a doorstop or coaster instead of that book there you could hardly put down.

Joe stops himself, embarrassed. Living off the grid of civilities, he's lost his manners.

But the woman is smiling. That's the kind of book I always dreamed of writing, she says. I once wanted to be a writer, she adds shyly. This was just meant to be temporary. She looks around the shop as if she has been held against her will by the cash register, the glass jar of jerky, the microwave, the stacks of napkins, the tray of salt and pepper shakers, the plastic containers of mustard and ketchup.

The next morning, Joe is back with a bag of his beans. They brew a cup. The woman's eyes widen with interest. She inhales the rich aroma. She takes a sip and smiles.

Where'd you get this? she whispers, as if there must be something contraband about such wonderful beans.

Joe tells her the story of how they came to be that good.

A better coffee, all right, she says, dumping the old beans into the trash. You know, she says, you should write that story down. Make it like into a book or something.

Your turn, Joe says, smiling. I told you the story, now you pass it on.

I can't, the woman says, wiping the counter extra hard, erasing some mark only she can see there. I need to earn a living, you know.

You need another cup, Joe says, pouring. Close your eyes for this one.

The woman closes her eyes.

When she is finished drinking, she opens her eyes.

I heard something, she confesses. The woman hums a song her mother used to sing as she put out a line of wash.

Joe smiles when the woman is done. Now turn your cup over. Let me take a look at what's ahead.

As he examines her cup, Joe explains how the old-time Dominicans read the future from the coffee stains.

I see you writing a book, he says, pointing to a scribbly stain. I see you coming to do research up in the mountains of a small island.

Joe looks at the woman and the woman looks back. There is a moment not unlike the moment Miguel once described on the mountain.

A B C

I was the woman behind the counter who wanted to be a writer. My life took a sudden turn when I met Joe, my husband.

This is really Joe's book, though he wouldn't want me to call it that.

We now live together on this mountain farm, surrounded by the trees Joe planted and by our campesino family. The coffee is thriving. The farmers are thriving. Everyone is reading. And I am writing!

One thing I've learned from the life I've lived: The world can only be saved by one man or woman putting a seed in the ground or a story in someone's head or a book in someone's hands.

Read this book while sipping a cup of great coffee grown under birdsong.

Then, close your eyes and listen for your own song.

As for this story, pass it on.

Afterword

by Bill Eichner

My wife Julia and I are not the man and the woman in the story, but our story is related to this parable. We do own a farm-foundation in the mountains of the Dominican Republic with caretakers, Miguel and Carmen, who live there with their children.

I am from farm stock in Nebraska. I grew up with a "bad cup of coffee." In the 1950s on the central plains, coffee was brewed from inferior beans, a brownish liquid so thin as to be sour and transparent. No doubt this custom of weak coffee was born out of the frugal nature of prairie farmers.

Julia is a writer who began publishing later in life. She grew up in the Dominican Republic, drinking *cafecitos* diluted with lots of milk—the strong brew was reserved for adults only. Six years ago the Nature Conservancy asked her to do a story on one of their protected sites in the mountains of the Dominican Republic.

While there, we were shocked by the "green desert" of the surrounding modern coffee farms. By the uniformity of the monoculture—hillside after hillside without a single fruit or shade tree. No sign of life except coffee plants and a single masked worker walking down the rows in a cloud of chemicals he was spraying on the coffee. I had not realized that the same kind of technification that had eliminated sea gulls and family farms in Nebraska was now doing a job on traditional shade-coffee farms in the tropics. Julia and I saw firsthand how globalization was changing the *campo,* or countryside, that we had both known as youngsters.

But there was hope. We met a group of farmers trying to organize themselves around growing and finding markets for their organic, shade-grown coffee. We sensed that they were battling an agribusiness trend toward growing coffee in full sun, for better short-term yields, while deforesting the mountains and poisoning the rivers with pesticides and chemical fertilizers.

We praised their efforts. They asked, would we like to join their struggle and buy some land before it was grabbed up by the big technified coffee plantations? Julia and I looked at each other—was it the mountain air, or our love for each other and for the idea of "giving something back"?—and said, why not?

When we accepted the invitation, we thought it would be a lark—develop five acres, raise a few bags of coffee to take home to our friends in Vermont, and sit in the *kiosko* with our *campesino* neighbors to discuss their plans. Maybe we could even build a little arts center on the farm, where our artist friends could come visit and share their talents with the neighbors.

As we became part of that mountain community, our goals changed. Our insights broadened with each step. We felt we should do more than grow coffee as a hobby. Why not model the process our neighbors were striving for? Our organic farm grew to 260 acres. We started planting heirloom varieties of coffee, and while the coffee seeds were germinating, we planted shade trees: a mixture of timber species that offered food for wild birds; fruit, nut, and avocado trees that provided food for us and the farm workers; legume species that added nitrogen to the depleted soil; and fast-growing trees that were pruned to provide forage for the milk goats and firewood for the *fogón,* or clay cookstove. Forest trees sheltered the tender coffee plants from the strong midday sun, dropping leaves to feed insects and worms that returned to the soil as it deepened and softened. The leaves caught the raindrops so they fell more softly on the earth, absorbing that rain in their root systems so that precious water did not rush down the hillside.

We also wanted to broaden our neighbors' concept of sustainability. Why should a farmer concentrate on acres and acres of coffee as an export commodity and meanwhile go down to the *bodega* to buy tomato paste? Why not grow tomatoes? Why not have chickens and goats and use the manure to fertilize the coffee plants, or plant citrus for shade and use the fruits for consumption and for sale at the local markets? Why not have a community garden and grow vegetables for the farm and the village? Why not start a composting system? Collect rainwater? Use solar panels rather than bring expensive electricity up into the mountains?

Our farm was transformed into a working school in which we all began to learn how to take care of the land and pass it on in good condition to the next generation.

From the start, our cash crop was shaded coffee as it has been traditionally grown in the area. But as we became more involved, we discovered that the coffee business is based on a culture of poverty where very little of the profit trickles down to the small farmer. In order to bring some of those profits home to the growers, the farms in our *cooperativo* pooled all our coffees together under the umbrella of CAFÉ ALTA GRACIA. We chose this name to honor the country's patron saint and protector, *la Virgencita de la Altagracia*, the Madonna of "high grace." We needed her blessing to help us aim high and to sustain us in the fight against the inequities of the coffee industry and the destruction of forests in coffee-growing lands.

As we worked to nurture the impoverished land, we could not ignore the human nature around us. The *campesinos* were living a life of poverty, and the most striking aspect of that poverty was that none of them could read or write.

We struggled with how to practice sustainability among those who lived and worked at the farm and in the community. We understood that our original idea of coffee sales supporting an arts center would be a kind of cultural imperialism until our workers and neighbors and their families could read and write for themselves. Only then would they have the key to unlock that treasure that belongs to all of us, the arts and literature of the human tribe.

Now a school building is at the center of the Alta Gracia farm. A volunteer teacher has joined the community. Kids and their parents are learning their ABCs. A youth group came from Wellesley, Massachusetts, and built a small library. We call it a *barra biblioteca,* modeled after a popular Dominican structure, the little *barra* at the side of the road where *campesinos* can get a *cerveza Presidente,* or a shot of rum. But our *barra* stocks books instead of drinks.

After five years, Alta Gracia has already been blessed with visible change. Organic matter is building up under the fruiting trees, rainfall is soaking in more slowly, the insects are returning, the *arroyo*s keep running a little longer each spring, and the songbirds come back every year to sing over the coffee. We look around the hills, and the green comes in varying hues and heights—from arugula in the garden or clover between the coffee rows to banana plants over our heads and *cedro* trees towering above all.

And books are arriving to fill the library. In time, we will also invite artists to come and contribute some of their time to giving workshops at the school or working on the farm. Total recycling. Wide-ranging sustainability. Taking care of each other through education as well as by what we put in the soil.

When I left my parents' farm as a young man, I never imagined I would return to farming later in life in a place so far from the center of the U.S.A. To farm on steep mountains instead of endless plains? To harvest crops in January rather than endure blizzards? To grow coffee instead of soybeans? And especially to enjoy a coffee that Nebraskans couldn't even dream of? In contrast to the family of my childhood, our poor and frugal Dominican family would never skimp on the "strength" of their coffee. They simply drink a smaller cup, yet rich enough to leave stains on the bottom and sides. I'm with them. I'll take two ounces of quality over a whole pot of bad coffee any day.

The tradition among the old *campesinos* is to turn their little cups over when they are finished. The future can be told from the dried stains left in the cup. Julia tells me that when she was a child, an old woman would go from house to house reading cups. If her fortune sounded good, Julia would close her eyes and wish that it would come true.

We have a wish: that others can enjoy the experience of our project and share in the dream and the effort of sustainability. Anyone can begin by planting a tree, or a hundred trees—the birds and your grandchildren will thank you. You can recycle and reuse until it becomes a habit that you teach others. You can buy and drink Café Alta Gracia along with other products offered by companies with a conscience. Remember, sustainability is not just a concept but a way of life whose time has come.

And whenever you drink coffee, remember this *cafecito* story. The future does depend on each cup, on each small choice we make.

A Better Coffee:
Developing Economic Fairness

Julia Alvarez's moving *Cafecito Story* is happily not just a story; it is now the living reality of half a million family coffee farmers around the world. These farmers and their partners in the marketplace—people that include Carmen, Miguel, Joe, and you, yourself—have turned decades of hard work and dreams into a powerful international movement called *fair trade*. Fair trade is about transforming the growing and drinking of coffee.

Fair trade is efficient and profitable trade organized with a built-in commitment to equity, dignity, respect, and mutual aid. Fair trade guarantees farmers like Carmen and Miguel

- direct sales for their cooperatives,
- a fair price, regardless of international market prices,
- improved access to credit,
- a long-term marketing relationship, and
- a commitment from buyers to support environmental sustainability.

We all want to end the human misery we hear about daily, but many of us find it hard to figure out what we can do personally. Fair trade helps us make a difference. It is a concrete step toward positive change. Buying fair-trade coffee gives you a delicious *cafecito* and the deeper satisfaction of knowing that you have helped farmers invest in health care, education, environmental stewardship, and economic independence.

And fair trade ensures that farmers earn a living wage so they can have the stability to provide a better future for themselves and their children. Helping farmers cultivate the courage to pursue their dreams helps us nurture the courage to pursue our own. Now isn't that a fair trade?

Shopping and Information Resources

In addition to coffee, you can now purchase fair-trade tea, gifts, clothes, housewares, crafts, and more. The resource listings here will help you make your own fair-trade partnerships.

U.S. Resources

Café Alta Gracia

758 Sheep Farm Road, Weybridge, VT 05753

Internet: www.cafealtagracia.com

The coffee cooperative founded by Julia Alvarez and Bill Eichner to bring a specialty coffee directly from the farm in the Dominican Republic to the retail market in the United States. The mission is to spread grace through sustainability—environmental, social, economic, and educational.

Co-op America

1612 K Street NW, Suite 600, Washington, DC 20006

Telephone: (800) 58-GREEN (584-7336)

Internet: www.coopamerica.org

Co-op America educates the public about the social and environmental consequences of purchases and investments. Their publications and online services help concerned consumers and organizations locate socially responsible companies and investment options. Check Co-op America's "Green Pages" directory for sources of fairly traded and organic goods.

The Fair Trade Federation

1612 K Street NW, Suite 600, Washington, DC 20006

Telephone: (202) 872-5329

Internet: www.fairtradefederation.org

The FTF is the national trade association of importers, wholesalers, retailers, and producers involved in fair trade with artisans and farmers around the world.

Global Exchange

2017 Mission Street #303, San Francisco, CA 94110

Telephone: (415) 558-9486 x245

Internet: www.globalexchange.org/economy/coffee/

Global Exchange works to increase awareness of fair-trade issues and to translate that awareness into consumer activism in the marketplace.

Oxfam America

26 West Street, Boston, MA 02111

Telephone: (617) 728-2437

Internet: www.oxfamamerica.org/fairtrade/

Since 1970, Oxfam America has worked to create lasting solutions to hunger, poverty, and social injustice around the world. Inquire about their fair-trade coffee campaign.

Seattle Audubon Society

8050 35th Avenue NE, Seattle, WA 98115

Telephone: (206) 523-8243 x13

Internet: www.seattleaudubon.org/Coffee/

This local chapter of the Audubon Society coordinates the Northwest Shade Coffee Campaign to create awareness about the connection between coffee-growing practices and threatened populations of neotropical songbirds.

Smithsonian Migratory Bird Center

3000 Connecticut Avenue NW, Washington, DC 20008

Telephone: (202) 673-4908

Internet: www.si.edu/smbc

This center at the Smithsonian Museum is a renowned source of information about research, educational programs, and publications concerning migratory birds. Visit their Web site to learn more about shade coffee–production practices.

The Songbird Foundation

2021 Third Avenue, Seattle, WA 98121

Telephone: (206) 374-3674

Internet: www.songbird.org

The Songbird Foundation's primary mission is the protection of migratory songbird habitat. They work with consumers and the media to publicize how fair trade sustains farmers who are the stewards of these habitats.

Specialty Coffee Association of America (SCAA)

One World Trade Center, Suite 1200,
    Long Beach, CA 90831-1200

Telephone: (562) 624-4100

Internet: www.scaa.org

The authority on specialty coffee. The mission includes promoting excellence and sustainability through sensitivity to the environment and consciousness of social issues.

TransFair USA

52 Ninth Street, Oakland, CA 94607

Telephone: (510) 663-5260

Internet: www.transfairusa.org

TransFair USA is the certification organization for fair-trade food products in the United States, part of an international network of certifiers. You can get a list from them of retailers in your area that sell fair-trade coffee.

Vermont Institute of Natural Science (VINS)

27023 Church Hill Rd., Woodstock, VT 05091

Telephone: (802) 457-2779

Internet: www.vinsweb.org

A nonprofit organization devoted to environmental education and research. A center for the study of migratory songbirds, their projects include tracking the Bicknell's thrush from its summer habitat in the Green Mountains of Vermont to its winter home in the "Dominican Alps."

Canadian Resources

Equiterre

2177, rue Masson, Bureau 317, Montreal, Quebec H2H 1B1
   Canada

Telephone: (514) 522-2000

Internet: www.equiterre.qc.ca/english/coffee

Equiterre is a Canadian nonprofit organization actively promoting certified fair-trade coffee in Quebec and other regions of Canada.

TransFair Canada

323 Chapel Street, Ottawa, Ontario K1N 7Z2 Canada

Telephone: (613) 563-3351

Internet: www.transfair.ca

TransFair Canada is the Canadian counterpart of TransFair USA. They can provide a list of retailers in your area that sell fair-trade coffee.

 This fair-trade primer has been prepared by Jonathan Rosenthal, co-founder (retired) of

Equal Exchange

251 Revere Street, Canton, MA 02021

Telephone: (781) 830-0303

Internet: www.equalexchange.com

Equal Exchange, a worker cooperative, was the first fair-trade coffee company in the United States and offers a full range of certified organic coffees and teas from small farmers' co-ops to caring people throughout North America. One hundred percent of Equal Exchange coffee is fairly traded.

One of the inspirations for *A Cafecito Story* was
Jean Giono's *The Man Who Planted Trees*
with wooodcuts by Michael McCurdy.
Chelsea Green published the first cloth edition in 1985.

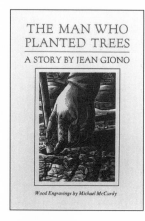

The Man Who Planted Trees

by Jean Giono
Wood Engravings by Michael McCurdy

Deluxe Cloth Edition

$16.95, ISBN 0-930031-02-4
6 x 9, cloth, 56 pages, 20 wood engravings

WoodWise Edition

A Special Edition with Co-op America's
WoodWise Consumer Guide

$8.95, ISBN 1-890132-32-2
6 x 9, paper, 80 pages, 20 wood engravings

Includes educational facts for young people and their
families about wood and paper consumption.

Note Cards

6 different wood engravings from
the book, blank inside

$8.95, ISBN 0-930031-78-4

Compact Disc

Music Composed and Performed
by the Paul Winter Consort
Narrated by Robert J. Lurtsema

$15.95, ISBN 0-930031-76-8

CHELSEA GREEN PUBLISHING COMPANY
800.639.4099 • www.chelseagreen.com

 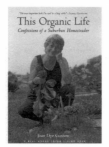 

ABOUT THE AUTHOR

JULIA ALVAREZ was born, as she puts it, "by accident,"
in New York City, but shortly thereafter her family moved
back to their native Dominican Republic. She spent her childhood
there until her family was forced to flee due to political pressure.

Her first book of poems, *Homecoming,* appeared in 1984.
Her first novel, *How the García Girls Lost their Accents,* was published
in 1990, followed four years later by *In the Time of the Butterflies,*
which became a National Book Award finalist. Her most
recent novel is *In the Name of Salomé.*

She is a writer-in-residence at Middlebury College. She lives with
her husband, Bill Eichner, in the Vermont countryside, but maintains
ties to her native homeland through their organic coffee farm
(Alta Gracia), established to demonstrate the ideas
and principles of sustainable living.

BILL EICHNER, an ophthalmologist by trade, comes from
Midwestern farm stock. He is also a gardener, chef, and the author of
The New Family Cookbook (Chelsea Green, 2000).

BELKIS RAMÍREZ, who contributed the woodcuts
for *A Cafecito Story,* is one of the Dominican Republic's
most celebrated artists.

A NOTE ON THE TYPE

A Cafecito Story is set in Galliard,
designed by Matthew Carter in 1978 based on the letterforms
of the sixteenth-century typecutter Robert Granjon.
The display font is Latienne.